MEXICAN
TEXTILES

MEXICAN
TEXTILES

SPIRIT AND STYLE

By
MASAKO TAKAHASHI

Introduction by
TONY COHAN

CHRONICLE BOOKS
SAN FRANCISCO

DEDICATION
To my father, Henri Takahashi, who valued art and artistry

ACKNOWLEDGMENTS

Special thanks to the weavers of Mexico, whose dedication and hard work have preserved the traditions of a timeless art. And to the following people, who were of particular help in making this book a reality:

Alejandro De Aguila, Rocky Behr, Marietta Bernstorff, Tony and Maya Cohan, Fidel Cruz and Margarita Mendoza de Cruz, Beverly Donofrio, Trine Ellitsgaard, Jeronimo and Josefina Hernandez, Sergio Hernandez, Gilah Hirsh, Cathi and Steven House, Vera Kandt, Kathy Lechter, Ruth Lechuga, Janice McCarty, Arnulfo and Mary Jane Mendoza, Remigio Mestas Revilla, Robin Mitchell, Francesca Passalaqua, Esther Ramírez, Carol Romano, Janet Sternberg, Francisco Toledo, Antonio Turok, Isaac Vásquez, Ronda Caleff, Jennifer Haas, Juan Macouzet, Veronika, and Michael Wineland. Thanks also to the gracious hosts of Las Bugambilias, La Casa de Mis Recuerdos, Hotel de la Noria, and Casa Oaxaca, who made staying in Oaxaca a memorable pleasure.

Library of Congress Cataloging-in-Publication Data available.

ISBN: 0-8118-3378-X

Designed by Brett MacFadden

Manufactured in China

Distributed in Canada by
Raincoast Books
9050 Shaughnessy Street
Vancouver, British Columbia V6P 6E5

10 9 8 7 6 5 4 3 2 1

Chronicle Books LLC
85 Second Street
San Francisco, California 94105

www.chroniclebooks.com

PAGE 2 Using a simple backstrap loom, an Amuzgo master weaver from Guerrero creates a technically complex brocade pattern that she knows by heart.

CONTENTS

INTRODUCTION

BY TONY COHAN

A glass pitcher, a wicker basket, a tunic of coarse cotton cloth. . . .
Their beauty is inseparable from their function. . . . Handicrafts
belong to a world existing before the separation of the useful
and the beautiful.

—OCTAVIO PAZ, *Seeing and Using: Art and Craftsmanship*

Every July, indigenous groups from throughout the state descend upon the Mexican city of Oaxaca for the weeklong folkloric festival of Guelaguetza, charging the streets with festive energy. Sixteen distinct Indian dialects spice the air; Spanish is a second language if spoken at all. The beautiful woven garments the women wear are encoded with art and meanings going back thousands of years. A queen is chosen—not the most conventionally beautiful but the one who most artfully represents her village and its traditional dress and speech. It's a soul-stirring experience to hear these women speak with pride and force of their origins, their traditions, the value they place on their customs and arts, and to see them parade through the streets in their stunning costumes.

At the women's weaving cooperative Sna Jolobíl, in the southern Mexican town of San Cristóbal de las Casas, a Mayan woman, dressed in skirt and blouse typical of her village of San Andrés Larrainzar, runs a credit card through a machine. Addressing the customer in Spanish, she folds the beautiful black wool jacket, woven in another nearby village, and hands it to the buyer. The transaction complete, the woman resumes speaking in her native Mayan tongue to her colleague, a woman weaving on a backstrap loom in the manner used for centuries.

At a gala opening at Oaxaca's Museo de Arte Contemporaneo, upper-class Mexican women, dressed proudly in exquisite *rebozos* (shawls) and *huipiles* (tunics) woven by indigenous women, sip *mezcal* and chat with students, curators, and

OPPOSITE **Stacks of colorful textiles showcase the rich textures and vibrant patterns characteristic of Mexican fabrics.**

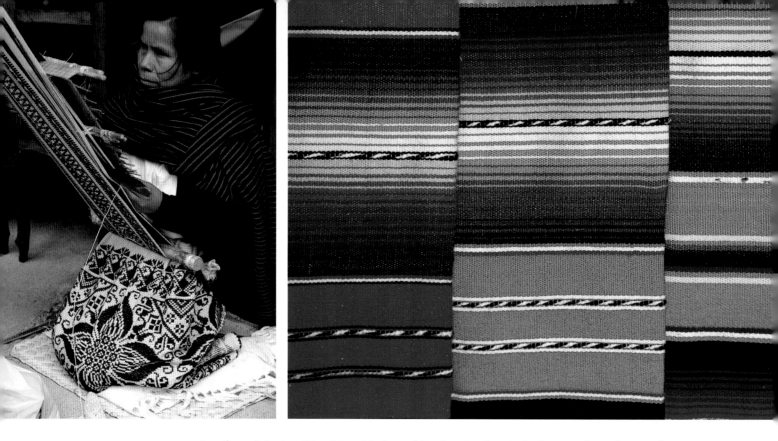

artists from Mexico City, New York, and Berlin. In the city's thronged markets and surrounding communities and villages, traditional artisans, wearing the very same clothes as the women at the museum, bring ancient weaving traditions forward into the new century, braving the onslaught of machine-made goods.

In Los Angeles, artists adorn their mid-century modern home with Mexican shawls from their collection, lending warmth to a cool, contemporary ambience. Across the country in a New York City boutique, a customer examines a handwoven Mexican cloth dyed a subtle red from the cochineal insect that feeds on the nopal cacti, imagining it as a table runner on her dining room table or perhaps as a hanging on her bedroom wall.

Handicrafts have not died out in our postindustrial age. Indeed they not only survive but flourish. Artifacts made by local artisans worldwide fill contemporary emporia alongside the latest synthetics and industrial products. Handmade furniture, baskets, pottery, and textiles decorate modern homes and offices. Travelers scour local markets in remote lands for the inspiration that only an object made by hand can provide.

The more technology invades our lives with impersonal, colorless, and "branded" objects, the more value we find in a beautiful handwoven textile. In ways we can't always describe, we mourn the loss of beauty and sensuousness in a merely functional world. Finding a lovely woven cloth in a Mexican market or in a shop in one's own land, selecting and purchasing it, blending it into one's environment as function or as decoration, bring aesthetics back into our lives—color, pattern, texture. Time slows down, if only for a moment, releasing us from our harried, hurried days; for it takes a long time to weave, and the result is something that only time can deliver. Woven objects also connect us to our own vanished histories; after all, who among us can't trace our origins back to ancestors who wove?

For many historical and cultural reasons, Mexico is one of the few remaining countries that still produces a wide variety of handmade textiles. The role of woven cloth in Mexico, strong since long before the arrival of the Spaniards, evolved in rich combination with European techniques for four centuries. Today, weaving survives in old and new forms, using both traditional natural dyes from indigo, sea snails, mosses, and tree bark, and modern synthetic threads and techniques.

Until the last century, Mexican women wove garments for themselves and their families. Nowadays, they make textiles to sell on the open market. While the contemporary world is coming to regard handmade objects as a way to connect with deeper values, Mexico's textile artisans on their end are adapting to the tastes and needs of their new customers. The women of Guelaguetza are proud of their weaving arts and would like to maintain them. For both maker and buyer, the purchase of a woven *rebozo* or *sarape* sustains and advances a living culture.

Mexican Textiles—fascinating, informed, and wise—celebrates, in photos and text, a rich and enduring tradition. It also brings Mexican textiles into the arena of contemporary life, offering us a way to participate in a culture in which beauty and function still coexist.

OPPOSITE, LEFT **Working on a backstrap loom, this weaver wears a blue and black striped *rebozo* shawl characteristic of *rebozos* woven in the state of Michoacán.**

OPPOSITE, RIGHT **Lightweight blankets, woven in graded stripes of color reflect the style perfected in vintage Saltillo *sarapes*.**

BELOW **Woven into the cushion cover are geometric designs inspired by ancient Zápotec patterns. A Guatemalan textile covers the bed.**

CLOTHING

IN MEXICO, THE HISTORY OF CLOTH IS THE HISTORY OF CLOTHING.

Mexico City's renowned Museo Nacional de Antropología houses dramatic painted murals salvaged from ancient pyramid walls, precious ceramics, and detailed pre-Hispanic stone sculptures, all depicting figures dressed in intricate costumes. The museum's second floor is devoted to extensive, three-dimensional displays of the lifestyles and costumes of more than fifty separate surviving indigenous groups. The dramatic continuity of clothing design from pre-Hispanic times is visible proof of an unbroken tradition.

Long before Columbus's arrival in the Americas, Mexico was home to a diversity of cultures—Mayan, Zápotec, Aztec, and many others—for whom clothing signified the status of the wearer. Aristocrats, priests, and warriors wore highly embellished cotton clothing, while the rest of the population wore garments woven from coarser plant fibers such as *ixtle,* henequen fiber from the maguey cactus. In colder areas, for added warmth, cotton was interwoven with brightly colored feathers or soft fur from the underbelly of rabbits. In the early sixteenth century the Spanish arrived and introduced woolens to the indigenous peoples.

Traditional Mexican clothing is woven on either of two types of looms, the oldest being the uncomplicated, portable backstrap loom. On the backstrap loom, the weaver stretches the warp (long) threads between two horizontal bars, one of which is fixed to a tree or a post, the other attached to a strap that goes around the weaver's lower back. The weft (cross) threads are then woven in. The length of cloth woven on a backstrap loom is almost unlimited, but the width is restricted to the weaver's body size. Backstrap looms are simple to assemble, yet many sophisticated weaving techniques can be used on them, including intricate brocading and tapestry. Clothing made from fabric woven on backstrap looms is traditionally pieced together from rectangular lengths of cloth.

Spanish settlers imported the second type of loom used to make traditional cloth, the treadle loom, which is a large wooden apparatus operated by foot pedals. They also introduced the spinning wheel, which spins raw fiber into yarn. These

OPPOSITE **A Tehuana dancer from the Isthmus of Tehuantepec pauses to pose in her remarkable embroidered velvet and lace gala costume.**

ABOVE **A Mayan vendor, protected from the sun by her *rebozo,* carries on the ancient task of selling corn, potatoes, and peanuts— all native to Mexico.**

two machines made weaving wide lengths of yardage possible. Scissors, also brought by the Spanish, allowed for more complicated patterns of garment construction to evolve.

Symbols woven into a woman's garment may represent much of her personal history, her rank in her community, whether she is married or single, the plants and flowers surrounding her village. The garment is emblematic of her. When an American folk art and textile collector saw a particularly beautiful *huipil* on an old woman in a market and asked to buy it, she told him, "I can't sell it. My husband died twenty years ago. When I die, how will he recognize me if I'm not wearing my *huipil?*"

Contemporary Mexican clothing, called *traje* (suit of clothing, in Spanish), originated in pre-Hispanic history, or they are *mestizo,* showing European/indigenous hybrid designs. The most widespread pre-Hispanic garments are the *huipil* (a roomy tunic), the *enredo* (a rectangle of cloth wrapped around the body as a skirt), and the *faja* (long sash). Among *mestizo* garments are the *sarape,* or poncho, a rectangular cloth often slit in the middle to insert the head; Spanish country-style shirts and pants for men; and skirts, blouses, and *rebozos* (long rectangular fringed shawls) for women.

Mexican women use the *rebozo* in imaginative ways—for warmth, as a child-carrying cloth, as a head covering, and to haul bundles. Traditional weaving centers such as Tenancingo in the state of Mexico and Santa María del Río in San Luis

  MEXICAN TEXTILES

Potosí continue to make meticulously crafted *rebozos*. Tying off the fringes is an art in itself, and the most elaborate *rebozos* take months to complete.

Today, in isolated rural areas, many indigenous people still proudly wear the clothing of their ancestors. While urban Mexicans dress in contemporary clothes, a growing trend among Mexican artists and intellectuals is to wear items of traditional clothing. Anyone lucky enough to be visiting the southern city of Oaxaca in mid-July during the yearly Guelaguetza festivities will see troupes of performers parading through the streets in splendid, diverse costumes representing their villages. An extensive artisans' market springs up in the central plaza, the zócalo, and flourishes there for many days. Vendors from all parts of Oaxaca bring their unique textiles to sell in this celebratory atmosphere.

These days, Mexican weavers are turning to the traditional weaving techniques they once used only for constructing clothing to make appealing decorative fabrics for contemporary homes. The subtle colors and textures of handmade fabrics are beautiful in ways that mass-produced textiles never are. Patiently spinning, dyeing, and weaving a cloth by hand ennobles both maker and buyer, imbuing each piece of fabric with an intensely personal quality and connecting us all to a vibrant human experience.

OPPOSITE **The Navarro Gómez sisters and their mother weave on backstrap looms in the courtyard of their village home in Santo Tomás Jalietza, Oaxaca.**

ABOVE **Contestants for Guelaguetza Queen. There are sixteen different ethnic groups in Oaxaca, and the queen is chosen for her overall knowledge of customs and traditions.**

THIS PAGE AND OPPOSITE **A busy family workshop in Oaxaca City, where generation after generation of weavers employ traditional wood pedal loom (sometimes called treadle loom) techniques, making cotton tablecloths and bed linens.**

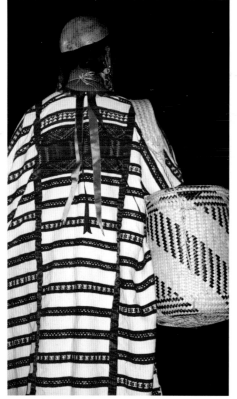

ABOVE **A Trique woman wears her traditional red and white** *huipil.* **The gourd protects her head from the sun and serves as a bowl when necessary.**

ABOVE RIGHT **A stack of naturally dyed, handwoven cotton shawls made on back-strap looms, commissioned by Artesanías Juanacata in Oaxaca City.**

RIGHT **An outstanding cotton Trique** *huipil* **dyed with natural dyes. More than six months of work goes into making a** *huipil* **of this quality.**

OPPOSITE **The pre-Hispanic double-headed eagle design on this Chinanteca** *huipil* **signifies an ancient belief in the duality of life.**

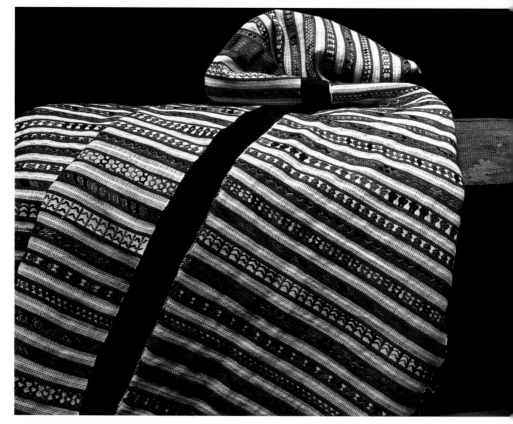

RIGHT **A *huipil* from Huautla de Jiménez, Oaxaca,** becomes an attractive wall decoration when simply hung on a dowel.

OPPOSITE LEFT **A Trique woman demonstrates back-strap weaving in the Mercado de Artesanías in Oaxaca City.**

OPPOSITE RIGHT **Trique *huipiles* offered for sale.** The best are of cotton, but many are produced in acrylic and are less expensive.

OPPOSITE **A woman wearing a** *rebozo* **remains a familiar sight in Mexico.**

LEFT **Sebastiana Rocha has been tying macramé fringe for fifty-two years, since she was eight.** *Rebozos* **are evaluated for the beauty of their intricate fringe, and those made in Santa María del Río, San Luís Potosí are famous throughout Mexico.**

BELOW **Two artists, Larry Pittman and Roy Dowell, use a** *rebozo* **as a table runner in their mid-twentieth-century modern home, designed by Richard Neutra.**

MEXICAN TEXTILES

OPPOSITE **This young woman from Zinacantán, Chiapas, wove and embroidered matching traditional costumes for her family with her own flair, making their clothing identifiably theirs alone.**

TOP **The glossy golden yellow *rebozo* frames a hand-embroidered velvet skirt from the Isthmus of Tehuantepec.**

CENTER **An assortment of embroidered Masateca blouses from Ayautla, Oaxaca.**

BOTTOM **Detail of the embroidery on a man's vest, from Zinacantán, Chiapas. Handmade fabrics should be treated with care; dry cleaning is recommended for the textiles on these pages.**

ABOVE **A detail of *Jaspeado*
(ikat), the weaving of a pattern
by tie-dyeing the warp, is shown
in a Santa María del Río *rebozo*
in progress.**

OPPOSITE **A young Trique girl
in her signature *huipil*, woven
with symbols expressive of the
Trique philosophy of the cocoon-
to-butterfly-like transformational
stages of life.**

TOP **A detail of Huichol cross-stitch embroidery.**

ABOVE **These thick-striped cotton *rebozos* are woven on backstrap looms by Mixe women in Tamazolapan, Oaxaca.**

RIGHT **Mariano Valadez Navarro and Josefina Candelario, Huichols from Nayarit, Jalisco, where men's costumes are decorated with finely cross-stitched embroidered symbols.**

TOP **This detail of cross-stitch embroidery on the yoke of a blouse is typical of the forest regions of Chiapas.**

ABOVE **A cluster of cushions made from cotton brocaded Mayan designs, handwoven in Chiapas.**

OPPOSITE **This handsome** *rebozo was* **woven of** *coyuche,* **a naturally caramel-colored cotton.**

LEFT **The ikat (tie-dyed warp)** *rebozo* **was woven by master weaver Evaristo Borboa; its fringe was expertly tied by Estonia Millán, both from Tenancingo, Mexico. The striped pillows are covered with Moroccan fabrics.**

BELOW **A mixture of textiles from Mexico combines easily with spangled Moroccan pillows.**

COTTONS

COTTON IS NATIVE TO MEXICO AND HAS BEEN CULTIVATED THERE since the beginning of recorded history. Luxurious cotton garments were highly prized as trade goods and valuable as tribute to the ruling classes. In the sixteenth century, the conquistador Hernán Cortés wrote to the king of Spain: "Moctezuma gave me a large quantity of his own textiles which, considering they were cotton and not silk, were such that there could not be fashioned or woven anything similar in the whole world for the variety and naturalness of the colors and for the handiwork."

Processing cotton by hand from its raw plant material into finished yarns is a time-consuming task, undertaken today by only a few dedicated craftspeople. After the cotton plants are harvested, the fibers are cleaned of seeds and other impurities, then spread out on a mat and beaten with sticks until ready for spinning.

Traditionally, women spin the yarns by hand on a wooden spindle. The smoothness of a plain weave fabric is determined by the evenness and consistency of the yarns used to weave the cloth. Even the very finest hand-spun yarns display a slight bumpiness in texture once they are woven, and running the hand gently over the surface of a cloth to feel for this texture is a test of whether a piece is indeed hand spun or not. Perfectly smooth cloth is an indicator of machine-spun yarns.

Traditional weavers use either a backstrap loom or a treadle loom to weave cotton cloth. Women generally work on the age-old, lightweight backstrap looms, while men operate the larger, freestanding treadle looms, which need greater strength to manipulate.

Mexican cottons once grew in many colors, and even today cotton grows in white (*Gossypium hirsutum*), a caramel color called *coyuche* (*Gossypium mexicanum*), and a pale green color that is almost extinct.

To dye cotton, artisans prepare traditional colorants from a variety of natural sources, such as crushed insects, plant materials, and the secretions of sea snails. Long ago, Mexicans domesticated the cochineal insect (*Dactylopius coccus*), which feeds on nopal cacti (genus *Nopalea*), for its impressive dye properties. Cochineal

OPPOSITE **Margarita Avendano of Pinotepa de Don Luis, Oaxaca, spins** *coyuche* **fiber. Her family specializes in** *caracol***, cochineal, and indigo dyed hand-woven textiles.**

ABOVE *Coyuche (Gossypium mexicanum)* **cotton grows naturally in this caramel color and is highly prized by collectors.**

Amuzgo weavers of Oaxaca and Guerrero grow, spin, and weave *coyuche,* a caramel-colored cotton fiber cultivated in Mexico. The brocaded designs are abstracted from natural forms, stars, lightening, insects, and flowers. *Rebozos, huipiles,* and table linens such as these are colorfast and can be hand washed.

production was quite important in Mexican history. When dried and crushed, the insects make a red dye that was once so cherished by Europeans that it ranked second only to precious metals, silver and gold, as an export item for the Spanish rulers of Mexico. Cochineal colored the military uniforms of the famous British redcoats and was the dye of choice until red chemical dyes were perfected.

The dyed fibers are then woven into spectacular patterns. Mexican textile design motifs develop from the weavers' mythologies and their perceptions of the natural world. Designs are passed orally from generation to generation without written patterns, and girls as young as eight years old learn to weave from their mothers. The agricultural Amuzgo people believe that scorpions attract much-needed rains, hence the popularity of scorpion motifs on Amuzgo textiles. A frequently seen design on Zapotec, Amuzgo, and Mayan textiles in Oaxaca and Chiapas is the horizontal diamond shape. Loosely translated, the four points of the diamond represent the cardinal directions of north, south, east, and west, and the center of the diamond is a window or door to the universe. On some garments, a diamond shape is worn over the chest area, signifying that the center of the universe is where the wearer is, at the center of her universe. When she dies, her soul exits through that door. Flowers and stars are other favorite designs. Today, the whole range of symbols is woven onto cotton napkins, table runners, place mats, and other useful items that are available in cooperative stores and markets in Oaxaca.

OPPOSITE TOP **Contemporary** leather *equipal* furniture is displayed with traditional hand-woven cushions at Icpalli, a home furnishings shop in San Miguel de Allende.

OPPOSITE MIDDLE **Simple** tablecloths and napkins woven from *coyuche* cotton are available in specialty shops in Oaxaca and San Miguel de Allende.

OPPOSITE BOTTOM **Animals** are favorite subjects of the Huave weavers of San Mateo del Mar, Oaxaca, and place mats such as this one are available in many colors in Oaxaca.

LEFT **Detail of a Mixe** *rebozo* available at Kojpete, an artisan's cooperative in Oaxaca City.

ABOVE **Traditionally, Mexican** weavers handle each step of the process from the beginning to the finished product. Here, hanks of yarn dry in the sun after being dyed.

BELOW **Cotton** *cambaya* cloth covers cushions in the contemporary living room of Sergio Hernandez, a Oaxacan artist.

OPPOSITE **The stripes on this traditional cloth from the coastal region of Oaxaca are dyed with vibrant cochineal and** *caracol* **dyes.**

BELOW **Hand-spun pink yarns dyed with cochineal. The lavender yarn on the right is dyed with** *caracol.* **Rare and costly, authentic** *caracol* **yarns are variegated in color and, when rubbed lightly, give off the scent of the sea.**

RIGHT **Shells of** *caracol,* **the sea snail,** *Purpura patula pansa,* **which is "milked" for use as a dyestuff.**

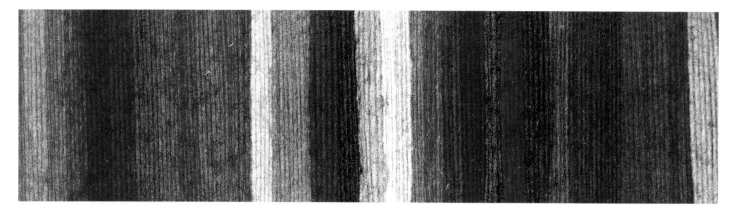

ABOVE **Cochineal produces a wide spectrum of colors.**

LEFT **When acidic lime juice is introduced, cochineal dye becomes blood red.**

BELOW **A cotton table runner, brocaded in cochineal-dyed raw silk, then splotched with** *fuchina,* **a colorant that bleeds into the surrounding fabric. This effect is much appreciated by the local populace.**

OPPOSITE **The nopal cactus hosts the cochineal insect. Only the female insect is harvested for its prized dye-producing qualities.**

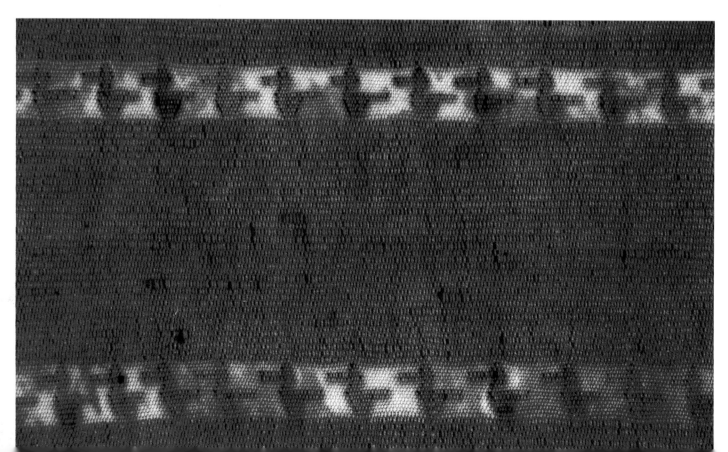

MEXICAN TEXTILES

LEFT **This selection of rare Amuzgo wraparound skirts features cottons dyed with indigo, cochineal, and** *caracol.* **From Pinotepa de Don Luis, Oaxaca.**

ABOVE **Indigo dye is made from the plant** *Indigofera anil.* **A small branch is shown here in a bowl containing chunks of dried indigo paste.**

BELOW *Anil,* **indigo blue, is a favorite Mexican color. Here it is used on the walls as well as on the cotton bedspread woven in Uruápan, Michoacán.**

RIGHT **Amuzgo weavers from Oaxaca and Guerrero create patterns abstracted from nature using backstrap looms.**

BELOW **An exquisite cotton *rebozo* graces a dining room table.**

OPPOSITE **Margarita Gill Francisco from Xochistlahuaca, Guerrero is wearing a fine quality, brocade-weave *huipil* that took over a year to make.**

ABOVE **A traditional Mexican papier-mâché doll rests among a collection of cushions covered in fabric woven in Chiapas.**

RIGHT **Originally woven into garments, textiles, like Chinantec cloth, can be transformed into cushion covers.**

OPPOSITE **A Chiapan textile left on a backstrap loom makes a striking wall hanging.**

MEXICAN TEXTILES

OPPOSITE **A selection of table runners woven by the Navarro Gómez family of women weavers. The figure at center is of *"El Danzante,"* a mythic dancer in Zápotec lore.**

RIGHT **Crispina Navarro Gómez, a prize-winning Zápotec weaver, in her village Santo Tomás Jalietza, Oaxaca.**

ABOVE **The terrace in Oaxaca's Bed and Breakfast Las Bugambilias is made inviting with a selection of locally woven cotton curtains and upholstery.**

LEFT **The subtle textures of white on white brocade weaving, distinctively Amuzgo, make lovely table linens.**

OPPOSITE **Hanks of yarn colored with natural dyes dazzle visitors at Tlapanochestli, a nopal cactus ranch where cochineal dyes are made.**

CHAPTER 3

WOOLENS

HIGH IN THE CHIAPAS MOUNTAINS, IN SAN CRISTÓBAL DE LAS CASAS, entering the marketplace surrounding the sixteenth-century Santo Domingo church is like stepping back in time. Highland Mayans from surrounding villages bring piles of handmade textiles to sell as they chat among themselves. The women, bundled in thick, feltlike wool skirts that protect them from the chill, wear symbols of their culture brocaded into handwoven blouses. The ancient symbols, transformed into patterns, signify the Mayan way of life.

When the Spanish conquistador Hernán Cortés arrived in Mexico in 1519, he made alliances with local groups hostile to the ruling Aztecs. Among these groups were the Tlaxcalans, who were granted special privileges for aiding the Spanish in conquering the warrior Aztecs. The Tlaxcalans of Apizaco, which was already a weaving center, were thus given the opportunity to produce woolens from the imported sheep they had learned to herd from the Spanish. Wool was first woven in Apizaco, in what became the state of Tlaxcala, in 1540.

Near the end of the sixteenth century, eighty weaving families from Tlaxcala were sent to Saltillo, in the northern state of Coahuila, to establish a weaving community there. Woolen Saltillo *sarapes* became famous for their rainbow-hued colors and delicate, refined quality, and the best ones are treasured collector's items.

Today in Mexico, inexpensive synthetic yarns such as acrylic and polyester are replacing wool in the production of blankets and garments. Still, some traditional woolen production continues in the cooler mountainous states. Woolen blankets, *sarapes,* and *rebozos,* made in much the same way as they have been for centuries, are woven in the natural tones of the sheep's wool, black, gray, and white, and in a variety of geometric patterns. Colors are obtained from natural sources or synthetic dyes, which are not shunned but rather admired for their vivid hues.

Around San Miguel de Allende, a charming colonial town in the state of Guanajuato once known for its textiles, a few remaining weavers make ponchos and inexpensive scatter rugs. Mitla, better known for its archaeological ruins

OPPOSITE **A Mayan weaver demonstrates ancient backstrap loom techniques in front of Sna Jolobil, a weaving cooperative in San Cristóbal de las Casas, Chiapas.**

ABOVE **The bustling textile market spills down the hill from the Santo Domingo church in San Cristóbal de las Casas.**

near the city of Oaxaca, is a center for weaving *rebozos*. Colorful and lovely as shawls, *rebozos* can be used as table runners or window treatments. Bernal, in the state of Querétaro, specializes in undyed, oversized, brushed wool shawls, which can also serve as lap robes.

Certain Mayan weavers of highland Chiapas concentrate on woolen production, and in addition to handsome tunics and jackets, they have begun selling woolen scarves and shoulder bags in the huge textile market of San Cristóbal de las Casas, which fans out from the Mayan weaving cooperative Sna Jolobíl (Weavers' House in the Tzotzil language). Exquisite, museum-quality textiles are on display and available for sale at Sna Jolobíl, which occupies a section of the stately, baroque Santo Domingo church. Master weavers demonstrate techniques as ancient as the Mayan culture itself, creating the designs passed down from weaver to weaver for thousands of years. Although many aspects have been lost, Mayan culture lives on, speaking to the future through its textiles.

PREVIOUS PAGES **Detail of the mounds of collectable woolen textiles stacked on shelves of Sna Jolobíl, the Mayan textile cooperative.**

ABOVE **An inviting sofa is decorated with woolen cushion covers and a** *rebozo* **from Chiapas.**

RIGHT AND OPPOSITE **Different views of two connecting rooms show how the use of woolen rugs and textiles from Chiapas and Oaxaca bring traditional touches to the colonial style bed and breakfast Casa de las Flores, in San Cristóbal de las Casas, Chiapas.**

◇ MEXICAN TEXTILES

LEFT **The soft woolen blanket on this antique daybed is dyed and woven in Oaxaca using merino wool yarns imported from New Zealand.**

ABOVE **This Mexican blanket's simple stripes complement the Indian and Moroccan patterned pillows.**

ABOVE **Spools of colored woolen yarn ready to be woven into intricately patterned rugs in Teotitlán del Valle, Oaxaca.**

RIGHT **The vintage Saltillo blanket and woolen Oaxacan rug bring warmth and color to a folk art collector's home.**

OPPOSITE **Evocative of Saltillo *sarapes,* this wool blanket is woven in Oaxaca of imported merino wool, then directly exported for sale by Santa Fe Interiors in the United States.**

ABOVE **A large woolen shawl thrown over a bed is from Bernal, Querétaro, where woolens are seldom dyed but left in their natural colors.**

OPPOSITE TOP **Natural wool shawls from Bernal, Querétaro are sold as sofa throws and lap robes.**

OPPOSITE, BOTTOM LEFT **A wool and cotton brocaded Mayan cloth adds a decorative touch to a leather-covered *equipal* table.**

OPPOSITE, BOTTOM RIGHT **A pair of dolls, dressed in traditional wool garments from highland Chiapas stand on a Oaxacan raw silk *rebozo,* and lean against a cushion covered in a wool fabric from Teotitlán del Valle.**

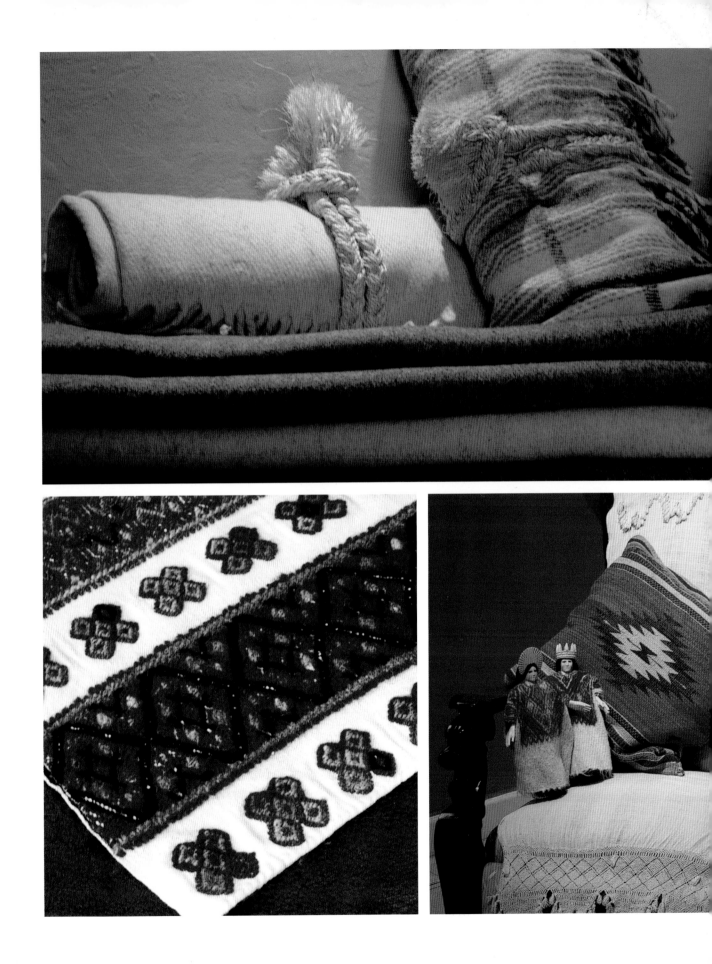

OPPOSITE **Vintage woolen Saltillo** *sarapes* **decorate a corner in the home of a collector.**

FOLLOWING PAGES **Naturally dyed woolen sarapes woven by Maestra Simona Yocupitzio Buitimez in her home in Navojoa, Sonora.**

OPPOSITE **A red woolen poncho is worn by a horseman in front of the parish church of San Miguel de Allende, Guanajuato.**

ABOVE **The young man's outfit is completed by the woolen *sarape* slung over his shoulder.**

LEFT **A distinctive woolen Mixteca *jorongo*, a *sarape* worn over the head, from San Mateo, Oaxaca, covers a vintage chest at the Hacienda Calderón in Calderón, Guanajuato.**

ABOVE **The Mexico City
living room of Ruth Lechuga,
features cushions from
Chiapas, and a blanket from
Michoacán.**

RIGHT **Ruth Lechuga,
distinguished author and
lifelong collector of Mexican
textiles and folk art.**

OPPOSITE TOP **Detail of a
woolen cross-stitched** *rebozo,*
**embroidered by Manuela Cecilia
Lino of Hueyapan, Puebla.**

OPPOSITE, BOTTOM LEFT
**This pre-Hispanic-style shoulder
bag rests on a matching wool
rug. Both were woven in
Teotitlán del Valle in a subtle
stripe pattern.**

OPPOSITE, BOTTOM RIGHT
**Bold, graphic designs distin-
guish these woolen** *sarapes*
**lined up for sale in Uruápan,
Michoacán during Holy Week.**

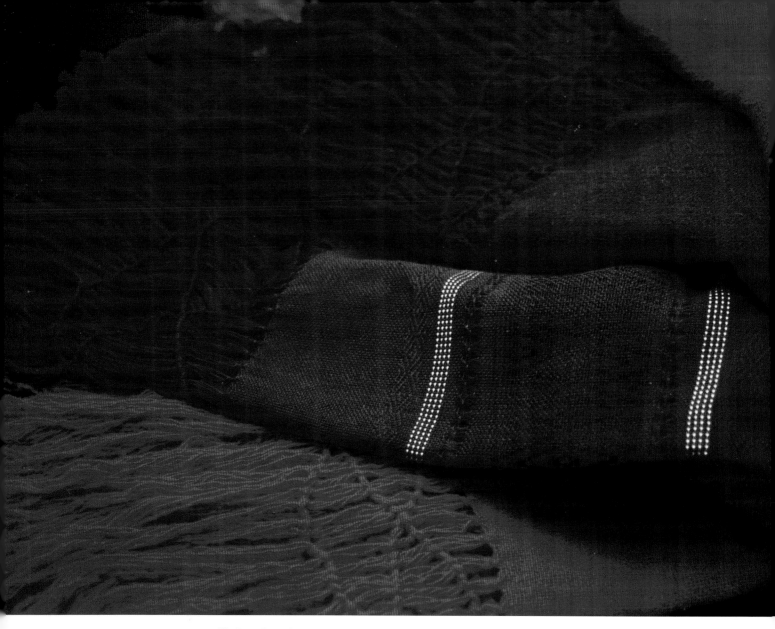

ABOVE **Woolen *rebozos* from
Mitla, an ancient Zápotec
archeological site as well as
a modern weaving village.**

OPPOSITE **A thick woolen
blanket is used as a rug in the
folk art–filled room of Casa
Luna, in San Miguel de Allende,
Guanajuato.**

CHAPTER

4

OAXACAN RUGS

EVEN FROM AFAR, THE VIVIDLY COLORED WOOLEN RUGS THAT HANG in front of stores and workshops along the road into Teotitlán del Valle, Oaxaca, appear like welcome signs. Each rug has been the focus of long hours of attentive labor by local artisans.

Historically, the indigenous Zápotecas never used rugs themselves. It is said that a Zápotec man, while working in Texas in the mid-twentieth century, saw rugs on the floors there for the first time. To him, they looked like thick blankets. He brought this revelation home to his ancestral weaving community, and the history of rug weaving in Oaxaca began. Teotitlán del Valle, a lively, ancient village in the hills near Oaxaca City, had already been a weaving center for many generations, making the transition to rug manufacturing a simple one.

Typically, the making of a rug begins with raw wool, which is cleaned, carded (brushed), and spun into yarn. The wool itself is generally from local sheep, or is merino wool imported from New Zealand (for its longer, softer fibers). Oaxaca has a mild climate, and its sheep do not grow hair as long as those from cold countries.

Many handsome rugs are woven using only the natural colors of the wool. Others are made with a variety of colors. Colorants are either natural or synthetic. Some weavers use synthetic dyes for reasons of economy. Natural dyes are time-consuming and exacting to use, but they produce traditional colors of depth and beauty—worth the extra work to the weavers and worth the extra cost to collectors.

Natural dyes are made from an assortment of organic sources. Pigment is extracted from plant material by boiling (and, in the case of indigo, fermenting the liquid) for hours, to make the dyes. Next, the yarns are immersed in steamy hot vats of dye many times until the desired color is achieved. The more frequent the immersions, the deeper the color becomes. Fixatives are applied to make the dye permanent.

As quality differs with each weaver, it is worthwhile to examine any rug before buying. Good-quality rugs lie flat, are tightly woven, and don't pill ("ball up" when

OPPOSITE **Baskets of natural dye ingredients and colored yarn samples are displayed on finished rugs at Casa Cruz, in Teotitlán del Valle, Oaxaca.**

ABOVE **Colorful hanks of yarn hang in the rug weaving workshop of Geronimo Hernandez, Teotitlán del Valle, Oaxaca.**

rubbed gently) or separate between the fingers easily. Whether their colors come from synthetic or natural dyes, neither should rub off on your hands.

Rug making is now the sustaining industry in Teotitlán del Valle and its environs. Most weaving workshops are Zápotec family-run operations. Generations frequently work together, sharing the tasks of dyeing, spinning, and weaving. They are proud of their work and will gladly stop what they are doing to demonstrate to visitors the various processes involved in rug making. Because rugs have always been made for export and trade, rug designs change with the prevailing tastes of the buying public. Famous paintings or Navajo rugs seen in books are commonly reproduced. Geometric designs influenced by motifs found on the nearby ruins of the dramatic Mitla pyramids are also popular.

Many workshops will weave custom designs from a drawing or photo. Patience and a willingness to experiment can be rewarded with a custom-made rug or wall hanging. Whatever the design, a handmade Oaxacan rug brings with it the sense of a culture that honors patience and the quality of work well done.

OPPOSITE **Rugs from Teotitlán del Valle and Santa Ana del Valle, both rug weaving villages, are displayed for sale at the Friday market in Ocotlán, Oaxaca**

ABOVE **Two generations of the Hernandez family work together in all phases of rug making.**

LEFT **Señora Hernandez cards wool by hand, a process of smoothing the fibers in preparation for spinning into yarn.**

LEFT **Precious cochineal insects feed and grow on nopal cactus at Tlapanochestli, a cochineal farm and dye producer outside of Oaxaca City.**

BELOW **Natural materials such as leaves, flowers, tree bark, mosses, and insects serve as rich sources for dyes.**

OPPOSITE **Señora Cruz Mendoza crushes cochineal insects, releasing a crimson color.**

PREVIOUS PAGES **Cochineal dyeing is carried out in clay pots over wood fires. Mexico is second only to Peru in the manufacturing of cochineal dyes.**

OPPOSITE **Samples of natural dye colors arrayed on a spinning wheel in the workshop of Casa Cruz, in Teotitlán del Valle, Oaxaca.**

ABOVE **Pink hanks of yarns dyed with cochineal hang out to dry, echoing the colors of blossoms in the patio of La Mano Mágica in Oaxaca City.**

LEFT **A sample of the many colors derived from local mosses in Teotitlán del Valle.**

ABOVE **Geronimo Hernandez weaves rugs to order in his workshop in Teotitlán del Valle, Oaxaca.**

LEFT **Chunks of dried indigo dye, called** *anil,* **require a labor-intensive process to produce rich blue colors.**

OPPOSITE **A selection of rugs woven in Oaxaca are designed and sold only at La Zandunga, San Miguel de Allende, Guanajuato.**

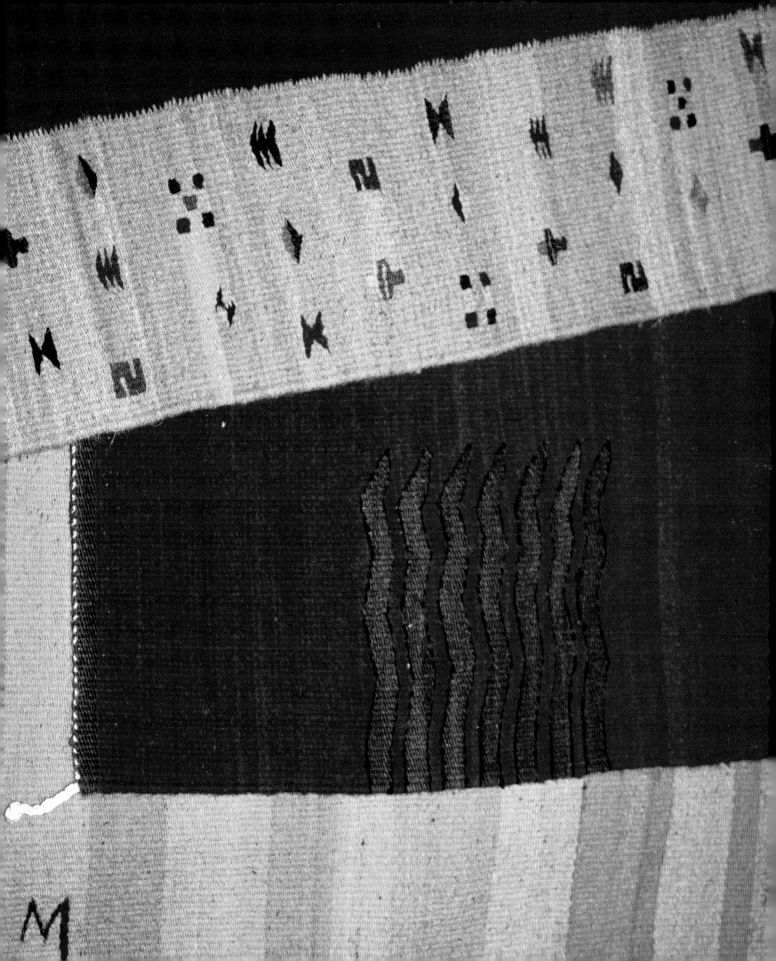

MEXICAN TEXTILES

LEFT **Oaxacan rugs and cushions add warmth and color to this sitting room.**

ABOVE **The classic Zápotec designs on this hand-woven rug bring traditional style to the contemporary environment of Casa Oaxaca.**

ABOVE **Isaac Vásquez, a master weaver of Teotitlán del Valle, at work in his family workshop.**

RIGHT **This tapestry appears to have been inspired by a photo of a cave painting. Many workshops will make rugs to order.**

OPPOSITE **A Navajo design was the inspiration for a large Oaxacan rug hung in a high-ceilinged den.**

ABOVE **Arnulfo Mendoza's work is inspired by historic Zápotec graphic design.**

OPPOSITE **A detail of an intricately woven museum-quality rug by Maestro Arnulfo Mendoza of Teotitlán del Valle, Oaxaca.**

ABOVE **"Musical Chairs," a rug designed by artist Mary Stewart, was woven in Oaxaca as a limited edition.**

LEFT **This naturally colored Oaxacan rug ties together the living room décor of folk art specialist Ramón Fusado.**

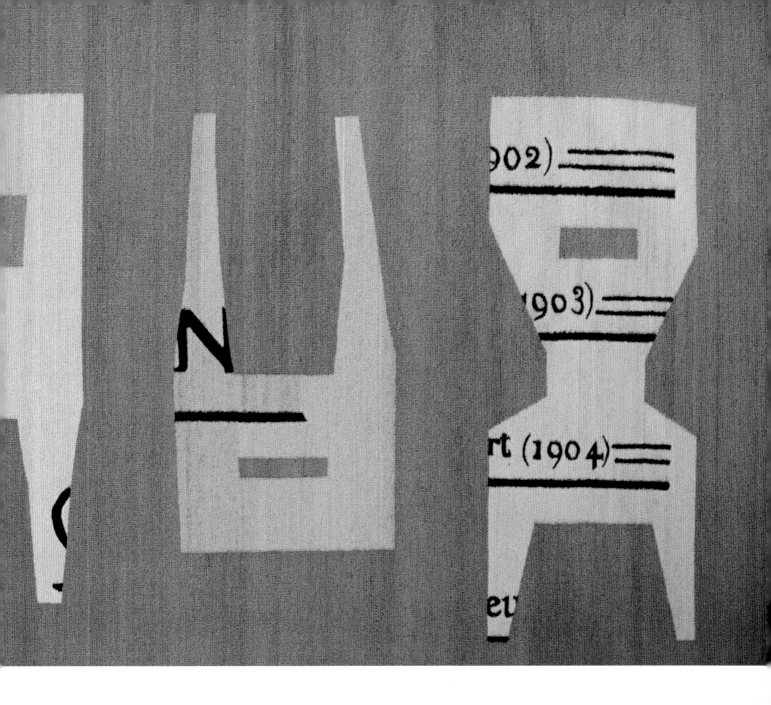

LINENS AND LACE

THE MEXICAN PAINTER FRIDA KAHLO, KNOWN FOR HER MANY SELF-PORTRAITS, frequently depicted herself dressed in extravagant Mexican traditional costumes. Often she wore sumptuous embroidered velvet and lace dresses from the Isthmus of Tehuantepec. The women of the Isthmus, an area on the southern Pacific coast of Oaxaca, are celebrated for their strength, pride, and command of their lives. Tehuanas, as women from the Isthmus of Tehuantepec are called, take great pride in their apperance and the beauty of their clothing.

Lace making began in Mexico to satisfy the demands of the Spanish settlers and became incorporated into Mexican decorative arts. Delicate place mats and tablecloths are crocheted, embroidered, or made with *desílado,* drawn-thread techniques. Certain nunneries support themselves by doing this work commercially. The town of Aguascalientes is famous in Mexico for the exquisite workmanship done there, but beautiful lace pieces are found in all parts of Mexico.

These days, particularly in the states of Oaxaca and Michoacán, traditional-style textiles are woven especially for use in interiors. Loosely woven curtain fabrics are translucent and delicate yet thick enough to afford privacy. In Oaxaca City, small workshops produce cotton bedspreads and table linens to order. The nearby town of Ocotlán has a lively cotton-weaving tradition and hosts a large open market on Fridays where goods are fetchingly displayed.

Rustic plain-weave cotton called *cambaya* cloth is manufactured in family workshops near Lake Pátzcuaro in the pine-forested state of Michoacán. Woven in a rainbow of colors, stripes, and plaids, the versatile *cambaya* cloth is washable and colorfast. For those who prefer it, there is a version in acrylic. The charming boutiques of historic colonial Pátzcuaro offer an extensive selection of bed and table linens.

The Amuzgo people of Guerrero and Oaxaca weave their ancestral magic into bedspreads, tablecloths, napkins, and table runners, practicing the time-honored backstrap loom techniques still used for weaving their traditional garments. Symbols of lightning, cornfields, stars, and other images of the world around them beautify even the simplest hand towel.

OPPOSITE **Women from the Isthmus of Tehuantepec dress in gala costumes and gather in front of the Santo Domingo church in Oaxaca City during the annual Guelaguetza festivities.**

ABOVE **Detail of the lacy dresses characteristic of native costumes worn by women of the Yucatan Peninsula.**

Mayan weavers have adjusted to market demands by adding cushion covers and table linens to their repertoire. The same significant iconography that adorns their *huipiles,* such as the diamond design that stands for the universe and its cardinal directions, can be found on cushion covers, place mats, and coasters in the huge textile market in San Cristóbal de las Casas. Mexican linens and lace pieces lend grace and depth to the contemporary home.

◇ MEXICAN TEXTILES

LEFT **Curtains and bedspreads woven on old-fashioned treadle looms are available in Oaxaca City, and at the nearby Friday market in Ocotlán. Cross-stitch embroidered pillow-cases are available in markets and cooperative stores in Oaxaca.**

ABOVE **The open weave of this typical Oaxacan curtain fabric allows the light to filter gently into the room.**

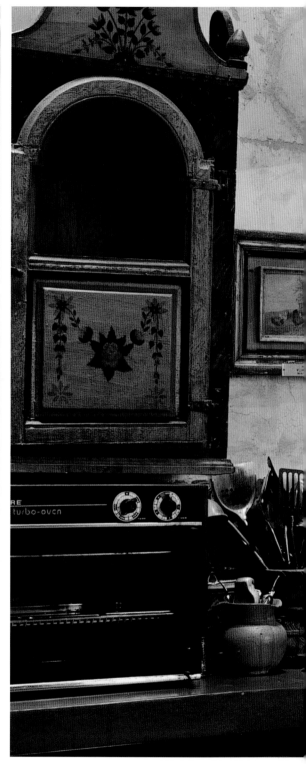

TOP **Charming pot holders in the shape of birds are made from cotton *cambaya* cloth in Pátzcuaro, Michoacán.**

ABOVE **This rainbow of colored napkins, each finished off nicely with macramé trim, is made from cotton *cambaya* cloth.**

RIGHT **The handsome country kitchen of the Hacienda Calderón, in Calderón, Guanajuato.**

LEFT **An informal dining table is dressed with country flair, using Mexican cottons and rustic, locally made dinnerware.**

ABOVE **Bright colors characterize Mexican linens and add a cheery note to this table.**

BELOW **At Las Bugambilias in Oaxaca, breakfast is served on layers of bright textiles.**

TOP **A selection of cotton table linens woven on backstrap looms in Oaxaca.**

ABOVE **A hand-woven napkin with a *coyuche* pattern woven in completes a table setting that features dinnerware embossed with pre-Hispanic symbols.**

RIGHT **This table is layered with hand-loomed textiles from Oaxaca. Loosely woven *rebozos* make beautiful curtains.**

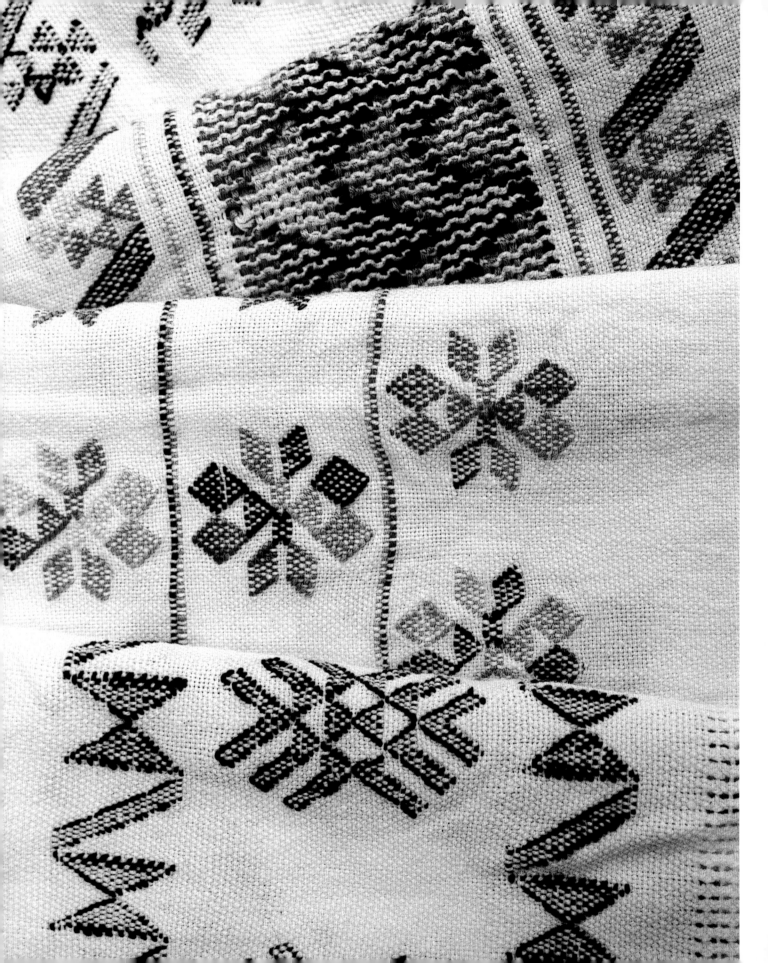

OPPOSITE **Hand-woven, brocaded tea towels made in Guerrero.**

TOP **Petals from the nearby bougainvillea sprinkle a patio table covered with a Oaxacan cotton cloth.**

LEFT **This custom-made cotton tablecloth was woven in Oaxaca as a birthday surprise for Carmen Fusado.**

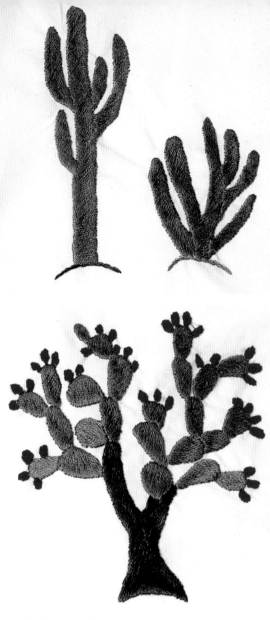

LEFT **The Camila boutiques commission nuns to embroider special linens for their shops in Mexico.**

TOP **The Mexican cactus motif looks fresh when embroidered on crisp white napkins**

ABOVE **A nopal cactus motif flaunts bright red cactus fruit, called *tunas*.**

OPPOSITE **A cheery collection of cotton tablecloths in the Friday Market in Ocotlán, Oaxaca.**

RIGHT **This traditional long red sash, used as a table runner, and the two coasters on it, are Mayan weavings from Chiapas.**

BELOW **Celebratory colors invite guests to relax and have fun at the Casa de Mis Recuerdos in Oaxaca City.**

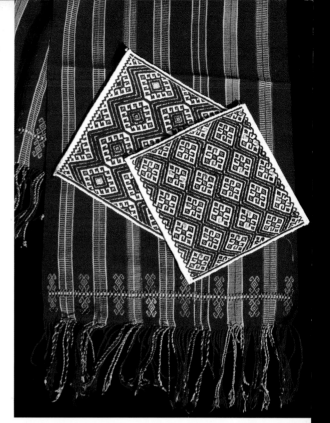

TOP **A sumptuous atmosphere is achieved by stenciling a lace pattern on the walls of this bedroom. Mexican and Guatemalan textiles adorn the bed.**

ABOVE LEFT **An amusing Mexican country scene is re-created in lace.**

ABOVE CENTER **Embroidered *servilletas*, or multiuse cloths, are made into cushion covers**

ABOVE RIGHT **Drawn thread-work, *deshilado*, is a method of making lace by manipulating threads in a fabric.**

OPPOSITE **A lace-making demonstration in Uruápan, Michoacán, during the yearly Holy Week Artisan's Fair.**

OPPOSITE **Beauty and simplicity come together in this contemporary Oaxacan home. The cotton gauze curtains soften the hard-edged lines of the architecture, and serve as mosquito netting in the rainy season.**

RIGHT **Detail of the curtain in its wrought-iron holder.**

The use of textiles in the Casa La Cuesta in San Miguel de Allende, creates an inviting atmosphere. The bedspread is from Puebla, the wall hanging above it is from Michoacán, and the *huipil* hung on the wall over the table is from Guatemala.

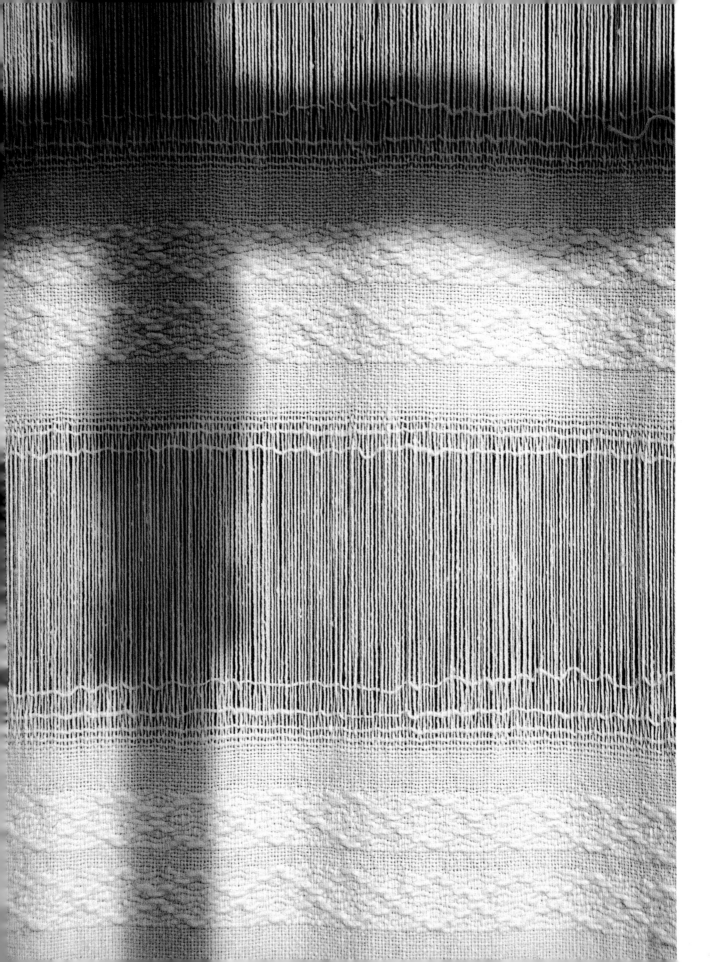

OPPOSITE **Detail of a locally made curtain in Oaxaca. The loose weave filters in soft light.**

RIGHT **Hand-loomed pillows from Chiapas add subtle texture.**

BELOW **These bed linens from Chiapas were chosen for their serene, neutral colors.**

SPECIALTY FABRICS

MEXICAN ARTISANS EAGERLY ADOPTED THE ELECTRIC COLORS of synthetic dyes and fibers, welcoming them into the Mexican palette when they became available. Sizzling, eye-catching colors are right at home in Mexican fabrics, evoking the bright floral colors found in nature.

Plastics are prominent in everyday life, but nowhere are they more colorful and enticing than in Mexico. Plastic netting is woven and sewn into shopping bags of varying sizes, shapes, and colors. Lightweight and pliable, the bags are strong enough to carry heavy loads. Thick plastic totes come in many sizes and brilliant color combinations and are replacing baskets made of traditional natural materials. Oilcloth, a practical, easy-care fabric, is ubiquitous in Mexico. Primarily used for tablecloths, Mexican oilcloth, in solid colors and showy prints, lends a carefree, picnic atmosphere to any table. Clever designers use it to make bags, aprons, and fashion accessories.

Hand embroidery is alive and well in Mexico. Women of Puebla work their satin-stitch magic on table linens. Embroideries from Michoacán depict scenes of local village life—fishing in Lake Pátzcuaro, farming the cornfields, and dancing the traditional dances. The Tarahumara people of Chihuahua sew three-dimensional fabric dolls in among their embroidered designs. The embroidered dresses distinctive of the village of San Antonino, Oaxaca, are so intricately made they are called *hazme sí puedes* (make me if you can).

Women of the Isthmus of Tehuantepec take special pride in their dress, the most lavish in Mexico. Even their everyday blouses are elaborately machine stitched with eye-catching geometric designs characteristic of the area. The beautiful floral designs thickly hand embroidered on their gala costumes appear to be inspired by the Chinese shawls originally imported by the Spanish on the Manila galleons in the seventeenth century. The square-shaped blouses can be easily hung on dowels for display or slipped over a cushion for instant color, when not being worn.

Hand beading is a specialty of the Huichol people who live in the states of Jalisco and Nayarit. The Huichol meticulously create beaded bracelets with symbols

OPPOSITE **A distinctively Mexican factory-made acrylic blanket, made after the design of earlier woolen Saltillo *sarapes,* now collectors items.**

ABOVE **This type of pictorial embroidery is fashioned in Pátzcuaro, Michoacán.**

ABOVE **Brightly colored striped blankets animate this art-filled blue bedroom.**

OPPOSITE TOP **In Oaxaca and Guerrero, elaborate beadwork is sewn onto the yokes and sleeves of women's blouses.**

OPPOSITE BOTTOM **The Huichol people of Jalisco make complex, beautiful beaded bracelets.**

from their complex philosophy. In Oaxaca and Puebla, glass beads are worked onto blouses and dresses as trim, framing the face with sparkling representations of nature.

These specialty fabrics reflect a passionate appreciation of color, pattern, and design. Traditional technique and modern materials are interwoven to create these vibrant and colorful Mexican textiles.

ABOVE **Fruit appears especially enticing when displayed on shiny, bright oilcloth.**

RIGHT **Vibrant, glossy oilcloth is popular all over Mexico, and the variety of patterns and colors seems endless.**

BELOW **A Santa María del Río** *rebozo,* slung over a mid-century modern chair.

RIGHT **A red** *rebozo* **is used as a table runner on an antique table, once a carpenter's bench, in the San Miguel home of Cathi and Steven House.**

LEFT **Printed cottons with large floral motifs are typical twentieth-century goods found in all regions of Mexico.**

BELOW **Cotton kerchiefs come in all colors, including these subdued examples used by designer Billy Goldsmith as napkins in a patio dining area.**

OPPOSITE **Mexican oilcloth covers a patio table in Southern California.**

OPPOSITE **Playfully rendered satin-stitch embroidery is typical of Puebla.**

LEFT **Amelia López from San Antonino, Oaxaca, is embroidering a difficult *"hasme si puedes"* (make me if you can) blouse.**

ABOVE **Detail of complicated, finely executed embroidery. There are many degrees of quality, and prices vary accordingly.**

ABOVE **A chair and ottoman have been extravagantly upholstered in a patchwork of Tehuana blouses.**

OPPOSITE, TOP LEFT **A Nahua woman from Acatlán, Guerrero, whose wraparound skirt features satin-stitch embroidery on indigo-dyed cotton.**

OPPOSITE, TOP RIGHT **Brightly colored birds and flowers contrast vividly with the black background of a cross-stitched embroidered *rebozo* from Michoacán**

OPPOSITE BOTTOM **Detail of a traditional Nahua women's wraparound skirt from Guerrero.**

ABOVE **This photo shows in detail the hem of a white bridal *huipil* made with feathers woven into colorful stripes. Only a few weavers alive can replicate these feathered garments first documented in letters from Hernàn Cortèz to the King of Spain in the early sixteenth century. The ancient weaving tradition is kept alive in Zinacantàn, Chiapas.**

OPPOSITE **Finely woven *rebozos* from Michoacán, feature an unusual fringe treatment reminiscent of feather plumage.**

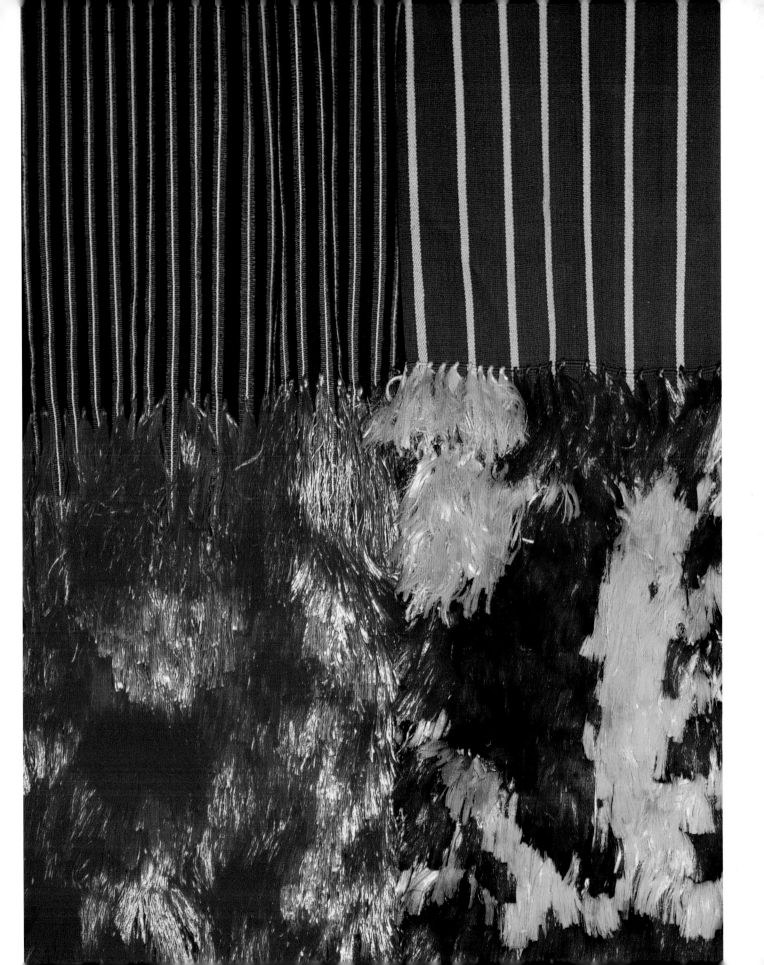

ABOVE **Purepecha embroiderers of Pátzcuaro, Michoacán, specialize in creating narrative pictures in cloth.**

RIGHT **Embroidered cushions portray village life. The one on the left illustrates Day of the Dead activities.**

SHOPPER'S GUIDE

Many traditional market days are still observed in Mexico. Highlights of the social calendar during Aztec and Mayan times, these same market days were described in detail by sixteenth-century Spanish chroniclers of the conquest. Market day is Saturday in Oaxaca City and Tuesday in San Miguel de Allende. Check with local tourist offices for schedules in other Mexican cities and towns.

BAJA CALIFORNIA SUR

INDIGO
Bulevar Mijares 6 B
San José del Cabo, Baja California Sur

GUADALAJARA, JALISCO

MERCADO LIBERTAD
A huge, rambling market in the heart of the city, where indigenous clothing and folk crafts are abundantly available.

CIUDAD JUÁREZ, CHIHUAHUA

FONART (THE FOUNDATION FOR THE FOSTERING OF HANDICRAFTS)
The government of Mexico promotes artisans by sponsoring yearly competitions and offering the public their wares. This is FONART's main headquarters and largest store.
Anillo Envolvente Lincoln y Mejía, Conjunto "Pronal"
Ciudad Juárez, Chihuaha
Tel.: (614) 613-6143
Fax: (614) 613-6458

MEXICO CITY

FONART
Avenida Patriotismo 691
Colonia Mixcoac
Mexico City, Distrito Federal 03910
Tels.: (55) 563-4060, (95) 598-5552

OAXACA CITY

ARTESANIAS JUANA CATA
Remigio Mestas Revilla stocks a large inventory of clothing made from traditional cloth plus a special line of naturally dyed garments.
Plazuela Adolfo C. Gurrion "D,"
Oaxaca City, Oaxaca
Tel.: (915) 514-3201
Fax: (915) 514-6926

CORAZÓN DEL PUEBLO
Good-quality textiles and folk art in abundance. Packing and shipping services available.
M. Alcalá 307
Oaxaca City, Oaxaca
Tel.: (915) 516-6960
Fax: (915) 516-7181
Email: corazon@spersaoaxaca.com.mx

GALERÍA INDIGO
An art gallery with rooms displaying fine-quality crafts and indigenous textiles.
Allende 104
Oaxaca City, Oaxaca
Tel.: (915) 514-3889
Fax: (915) 514-8338
Email: info@indigo.org.mx

LA MANO MÁGICA

*Rugs and tapestries by Arnulfo Mendoza,
assorted textiles and folk art.*
M. Alcalá 203
Oaxaca City, Oaxaca
Tel./Fax: (915) 516-4275
Email: manomagica@spersaoaxaca.com.mx

LIBRERÍA GRAÑEN PORRUA

*A bookstore, café, and boutique with a selection
of high-quality textiles.*
M. Alcalá 10
Oaxaca City, Oaxaca
Tel.: (915) 516-9901, (915) 516-8038

**MARO (REGIONAL ASSOCIATION OF
CRAFTSWOMEN OF OAXACA)**

*Huge assortment of native costumes, table
linens, rugs, and crafts, made and sold by
members of a women's cooperative.*
5 de Mayo 204
Oaxaca City, Oaxaca
Tel./Fax: (915) 546-0670

EMILIA TEXTILES

*Lots of inventory plus custom-made curtains
and table linens.*
García Vigil 512-A
Oaxaca City, Oaxaca
Tel.: (915) 516-6685
Fax: (915) 514-9403
Email: edna1110@prodigy.net.mx
Website: http://www.intercys.com/emilia-
textiles

**KOJPETE, TEJEDORES DE VIDA
(WEAVERS OF LIFE)**

*Hand-loomed textiles from the small Mixe
village of Santa Maña Tlahuitoltepec, Oaxaca.*
Murguía, near the corner of 5 de Mayo,
Oaxaca City, Oaxaca
Tel.: (915) 514-8694
Email: artesanias@tlahui.bicap.edu.mx
Website: http://www.bicap.edu.mx

TEXTILES OROZCO

A family workshop producing bedspreads and table linens to order.
Santo Tomás 214
Barrio de Xochimilco
Oaxaca City, Oaxaca
Tel.: (915) 515-2332

ARIPO

The state of Oaxaca sponsors this showcase of locally made traditional garments, handwoven textiles, and folk arts.
García Vigil 809
Oaxaca City, Oaxaca
Tel.: (915) 514-4030
Fax: (915) 514-0861

TLAPANOCHESTLI, COLORANTES NATURALES DE OAXACA

Nopal ranch and cochineal dye manufacturer with small gift store. Tours by appointment.
Rancho La Nopalera
Coyotepec, Oaxaca
Tel.: (915) 551-0030
Fax: (915) 551-0053

FONART

Crespo 114
Oaxaca City, Oaxaca
Tel./Fax: (915) 516-5764

MERCADO BENITO JUÁREZ

The large market two blocks south of the zócalo in Oaxaca City where many vendors sell traditional clothing, textiles, and crafts. The following vendors specialize in authentic indigenous textiles.

"OAXACA AND ITS REGIONS"

Crispín Morales Osorio mans one of the two oldest booths specializing in indigenous textiles in the Juárez market.
Mercado Benito Juárez, 230 (348)
Tel.: (915) 514-0859

"ADRIANA"

Enríque León López is in charge of the other long-established shop featuring a large assortment of excellent-quality traditional costumes.
Mercado Benito Juárez, 365 and 366
Tel.: (915) 516-0239

RICARDO RODRIGUEZ

At the central north entrance, Ricardo Rodríguez has a large selection of blankets, rugs, sarapes, and traditional garments.
Mercado Benito Juárez, 13
Tel. (915) 516-1318

MERCADO DE LAS ARTESANIAS

Located southwest of the Mercado Benito Juárez, this entire market is filled with vendors selling handcrafted textiles, mostly from Oaxaca and nearby Chiapas. Friendly bargaining is expected.

OCOTLÁN, OAXACA

Market day is Friday, and this busy market fills the tree-lined colonial plaza adjacent to the restored church and museum in the center of town. Cotton bed and table linens are loomed in Ocotlán and are prominently for sale. This market is so popular that rug sellers from Teotitlán del Valle bring their wares.

CRISPINA NAVARRO GÓMEZ AND HER FAMILY OF WOMEN WEAVERS

Benito Juárez 42
Santo Tomás Jalietza, Ocotlán, Oaxaca

PÁTZCUARO, MICHOACÁN

CASA DE LAS ONCE PATIOS

This shopping mall is located in a rambling colonial mansion with eleven patios in the center of town. Each patio is edged with shops, several of which feature cotton *cambaya* cloth items for sale.

DON VASCO BAZAR

One of several boutiques lining the central plaza featuring locally made table and bed linens.
Plaza Vasco de Quiroga 34
Pátzcuaro, Centro, Michoacán
Tel. (434) 342-0527

SAN CRISTÓBAL DE LAS CASAS, CHIAPAS

The daily outdoor market around the Santo Domingo church is bustling with vendors selling mostly textiles.

SNA JOLOBÍL

An exceptional weaving cooperative showing museum-quality Mayan garments and textiles.
Calzada Lázaro Cárdenas 42
San Cristóbal de Las Casas, Chiapas
Tel./Fax: (961) 678-2646

SOCIEDAD COOPERATIVA UNIÓN REGIONAL DE ARTESANOS DE LOS ALTOS DE CHIAPAS

A weaving cooperative featuring garments and textiles from the area. Across from the Santo Domingo church.
Avenida General Utrillo 43
San Cristóbal de Las Casa, Chiapas
Tel.: (961) 678-2848

SAN LUIS POTOSÍ, SAN LUIS POTOSÍ

FONART

Jardín Guerrero 6
San Luis Potosí, San Luis Potosí
Tel./Fax: (444) 812-7521

SAN MIGUEL DE ALLENDE, GUANAJUATO

VERYKA

Museum-quality folk art and a carefully selected group of indigenous textiles.
Zacateros 6-A
San Miguel de Allende, Guanajuato
Tel.: (415) 152-2114

LA ZANDUNGA

The rugs here are woven in Oaxaca but designed in San Miguel de Allende by Rebeca Kamelhar de Gutiérrez.
Hernández Macias 129
San Miguel de Allende, Guanajuato
Tel./Fax: (415) 152-4608
Email: zandunga@prodigy.net.mx

TAPETES EL TELAR

Decorative handwoven rugs and blankets sold wholesale and retail.
Salida a Celaya 19
San Miguel de Allende, Guanajuato
Tel.: (415) 152-1845

CASAS COLONIALES

A home furnishings shop with a variety of table and bed linens, many from Oaxaca.
Canal 36
San Miguel de Allende, Guanajuato
Tel: (415) 152-0286

CASA MAXWELL

This general store within a colonial mansion has a selection of rebozos from all over Mexico, table linens, and a separate room featuring cotton cambaya cloth for use in interior decorating.
Canal 14 and Umarán 3
San Miguel de Allende, Guanajuato
Tel./Fax: (415) 152-0247
Email: maxwellm@prodigy.net.mx
Website: http://www.maxwell.freeservers.com

NUEVO MUNDO

A carefully selected group of textiles and folk art in a charming setting.
Facing the San Francisco Church entrance, San Miguel de Allende, Guanajuato

SÁVIA

A small but choice collection of textiles and folk art.
Calle Jesus 12
San Miguel de Allende, Guanajuato
Tel./Fax: (415) 154-4866
Email: savia@indigo.org.mx

ICPALLI

Contemporary home furnishings designed with traditional materials.
Recreo 8-B
San Miguel de Allende, Guanajuato
Tel.: (415) 152-1236

CASA ANGUIANO

Cotton cambaya cloth yardage and traditional clothing sold here, along with a variety of other locally made crafts.
Corner of Canal and Hernandez Macias
San Miguel de Allende, Guanajuato
Tel.: (415) 152-0107

TALISMAN

A clothing boutique featuring exquisite rebozos from Santa María del Río and Tenancingo.
San Francisco 7
San Miguel de Allende, Guanajuato
Tel.: (415) 152-0438

CAMILA

Fine-quality embroidery and lace table linens.
Recreo 8
San Miguel de Allende, Guanajuato
Tel.: (415) 152-7754

SANTA MARÍA DEL RÍO, SAN LUIS POTOSÍ

On the main square of this small village is a rebozo weaving school that is open to the public.

SALA DE EXHIBICIÓN Y VENTAS

A weaving cooperative with a selection of beautiful rebozos made in local family workshops.
Pascual M. Hernández 120
Jardín Hidalgo
Santa María del Río, San Luis Potosí
Tel./Fax: (444) 853-0894
Email: Odfsantamaria@hotmail.com

TEOTITLÁN DEL VALLE, OAXACA

TALLER ISAAC VÁSQUEZ, "THE BUG IN THE RUG"

Master weaver Isaac Vásquez and his family workshop specialize in rugs woven with color-fast natural dyes.
Avenida Hidalgo 30
Teotitlán del Valle, Oaxaca
Tel.: (915) 524-4122

CASA CRUZ, FIDEL CRUZ LAZO

Proprietor Fidel and his wife, Luisa, weave and sell rugs and will take special orders.
Avenida Juárez km 2
Teotitlán del Valle, Oaxaca
Tel.: (915) 521-4020

CASA VÁSQUEZ

Ernesto and Margarita gladly demonstrate spinning and weaving techniques in their spacious showroom located on the road entering the town.
Teotitlán del Valle, Oaxaca
Tel.: (915) 524-4144